Wheels Around Ayrshire

by
Robert Grieves

Burns' Cottage at Alloway was quite naturally a popular location for picture postcard views (see also page 6) and publicity photographs. This scene in 1951 was taken to publicise the latest coaches operated on the Glasgow–London express by Western SMT of Kilmarnock, to compete with Northern Roadways of Glasgow, their rival on the service. HWS 935 was one of 14 similar underfloor-engined AEC Regal IV chassis with 30-seat Alexander coachwork which were the mainstay of the London service from their delivery in 1951 until Guy Arab centre-entrance coaches started to replace them in 1954. These AECs took the place of the remaining half-cab Leylands which had previously operated the London route in the late 1940s. On withdrawal from long-distance duties, the AECs had their seating capacity increased and were downgraded to dual-purpose and service work.

"LOUDOUN" LADY'S No. 1.

Cycles! CYCLES! Cycles!

We are Makers. Bicycles built to Order.

REPAIRS OF ALL KINDS Promptly and Cheaply Executed.

Nickel-Plating and Enamelling.

The "Loudoun" Cycle Co.,

18 and 20 WELLINGTON STREET, Kilmarnock.

© Robert Grieves 2001
First published in the United Kingdom, 2001,
by Stenlake Publishing, Ochiltree Sawmill, The Lade,
Ochiltree, Ayrshire, KA18 2NX
Telephone / Fax: 01290 423114
www.stenlake.co.uk

ISBN 1 84033 146 1

Left: In the Edwardian era, and also in the previous Victorian days, the main means of getting about locally apart from walking was to go by bicycle. Travel by train was often possible for longer distances but regular bus services were not available until around the mid-1920s. Few folks owned a private car, which was the prerogative of the upper classes during the first few decades of the twentieth century. Really it was not until the 1950s that cars became a financial possibility for many. As a result, cycle dealers multiplied in the first few years of the 1900s and many built their own brand of bike. This Edwardian advert was for one such company, John Campbell's 'Loudoun' Cycle Co. of Wellington Street, Kilmarnock.

Opposite: In the 1920s, few working and middle-class folk could afford the luxury of a family car. Motorcycles were popular and this New Hudson of 1929 was the pride and joy of John Barr who lived in Dreghorn. John and his brother Willie were both well-known local bus drivers who were employed by a variety of Ayrshire companies during the 1920s, and later ended their working lives with the giant Western SMT Company. This motorcycle carried the Ayrshire registration number AG 4468. The 'AG' letters commenced in November 1925, replacing Ayrshire's original 'SD' letters which had reached 9999 following their inception in 1904 when motor vehicle license letters were introduced throughout the British Isles. When 'AG' reached its maximum in May 1934 'CS' then started. Later, of course, prefix initials were introduced to give three-letter index marks.

INTRODUCTION

Historically, Ayrshire holds a number of important early connections relative to wheels, transport and roads. For instance, John Boyd Dunlop, who was born in Dreghorn in 1839, started his working life as a vet, but is better remembered for having developed and perfected the pneumatic tyre (another Scotsman – Robert Thomson from Stonehaven – was its inventor). In Dublin in 1890, Dunlop opened the first factory in the world to manufacture pneumatic tyres. The magnitude of his contribution to motoring is beyond doubt – especially the increase in speed and comfort made possible by the pneumatic tyre.

An earlier son of Ayrshire was William Murdoch, born in 1754 at Lugar and who apart from having invented gas lighting was generally a brilliant engineer whose other achievements were largely overshadowed. While working for James Watt in Cornwall during the 1780s, Murdoch developed a steam-driven carriage but was persuaded to abandon the project. Many of William Murdoch's skills were no doubt inherited from his father, John, who was no mean inventor himself. Around 1770, he had developed a crude bicycle, one stage better than the existing 'hobby horse' types, which were moved along by the rider's feet contacting the ground. John Murdoch 'cycled' between Lugar and Cumnock on his two-wheeled invention which he propelled by poles. Remember this took place long before 1839 when Kirkpatrick MacMillan in neighbouring Dumfries-shire at Keir Smiddy, by Penpont, perfected the world's first proper pedal cycle.

Another important lad born in Kyle, as regards the roads over which our wheeled transport must ply, was John Loudon McAdam (1756–1836) from Ayr, who concerned himself with the materials and methods used in road-making and is remembered today by the terms 'macadamising' and 'tarmacadam'.

Ayrshire could also boast Scotland's earliest railway, or tram-road, a 4' gauge double track constructed to carry coal from Kilmarnock to Troon harbour by local landowner William Henry Cavendish-Bentinck, Marquis of Titchfield and later 4th Duke of Portland. It was also used to carry passengers from the time of its opening in July 1812, normally in horse-drawn open wagons, but the line briefly saw steam operation as early as 1817 when the George Stevenson-built loco, the *Duke*, was used for a few years. A four-arched stone bridge (Laigh Milton viaduct) was built to carry the line over the River Irvine near Gatehead, and although no longer in use is reckoned to be the world's oldest railway viaduct.

Ayrshire's railway town, of course, has always been Kilmarnock. Today, however, Andrew Barclay (now Hunslet–Barclay) is the only locomotive builder remaining in the town (and in Scotland even) from several other once-familiar railway names such as Allan Andrews & Co., Barr, Morrison & Co., the Kilmarnock Engineering Co. Ltd., Dick, Kerr & Co., McCulloch & Kennedy Ltd., and Grant, Ritchie & Co. The Glasgow & South Western Railway Company also designed and built their own locomotives in their Bonnyton workshops.

Readers will notice that the majority of the photographs of buses and commercial vehicles in this book depict examples built by Albion Motors of Scotstoun, Glasgow. This is not simply a coincidence as it was quite natural for this make to outsell its rivals in Ayrshire and indeed Scotland as a whole. The Scotstoun works were relatively close to the county and its products were fine examples of engineering – ruggedly built and with a reputation for reliability (the Albion motto was *Sure as the Sunrise*). Prices, too, were competitive with those of other manufacturers and so it is not surprising that this make was so popular. In later years, however, Ayrshire had its own commercial vehicle builders. Massey–Harris (later Massey–Ferguson) tractors were built in Kilmarnock, Volvo–Ailsa trucks and buses in Irvine, and Stonefield specialist vehicles in Cumnock.

'Everything but the kitchen sink' would perhaps be appropriate to describe this scene of a horse-drawn wagon performing a Kilmarnock flitting in the late 1890s. The horse appears quite content munching the contents of its nosebag but the men loading the various household items seem to have had a tricky task balancing everything safely. The carter to the rear is holding a length of rope in his left hand while mopping his brow with his right and a sofa on the pavement has still to be loaded aboard. Perhaps the two boys, the younger of whom is barefoot, are members of the flitting family. They appear to be anxiously observing the proceedings. At this period there were several local carriers in Killie including Donald Aitken, Matthew Bryson, Peter McCall and David Wilson, but the owner of this wagon is not known. The location is West Langlands Street, looking down the brae towards John Finnie Street and these buildings are long demolished.

Main Street, Dunlop

The apparently unhurried manner of living one hundred years ago is conveyed in this tranquil glimpse of village life in the then sleepy community of Dunlop. This scene in Main Street about 1902 suggests that stress was not a concern to either the local grocer, seen in long apron at his shop doorway below a sign advertising 'Mazzawattee Tea', or indeed to any of his prospective customers. Wheels in this view are provided by the horse-drawn cart, probably from one of the many local farms engaged in dairying and cheese production. This scene today in what is now mainly a commuter village, with many of the population travelling daily by train or car to Glasgow, is relatively unchanged although the shop (latterly a draper's) has now been converted to dwellings.

An early Edwardian scene in Largs Main Street at the Station Square. Motor traffic at this time was almost non-existent and the few cars around were generally owned by the well-to-do, since the purchase of an automobile was considerably beyond the means of most families. As a result, the railways carried the majority of the population on longer journeys and alternatively until the first bus services were operational people either walked or cycled. Additionally, several horse-drawn charabancs operated from Largs since the coastal resort attracted many visitors. This was probably one of Watson's 'charas' about to depart with a full complement for Fairlie.

This postcard view of Alloway shows the famous Burns' Cottage in early Edwardian days with what was then one of the new Ayr Corporation tramcars (no. 8) passing fully-loaded on its way from Prestwick Cross on the main cross-town service to the terminus at Burns' Monument on a fine summer afternoon. Ayr's municipal tramway system had officially opened in September 1901 and the first 10 cars then in use were built by Hurst, Nelson & Co. Ltd. of Motherwell, as were the majority of the others which followed over the years. The trams were painted in a dignified dark chocolate livery with the town crest applied on each side and relieved by cream lower side panels. Advertisements usually adorned both sides and ends of the upper deck and in the case of no. 8 were for Glasgow-made 'Palomine' cigarettes at 20 for 6d and Limond's mangles and wringers. (Thos. Limond owned a thriving ironmongery and hardware store in Ayr High Street.)

Kilmarnock council kept up with their neighbouring municipal Joneses at the coast by introducing their own tramway system in 1904, three years after Ayr. Seen here is Kilmarnock Corporation Tramways car no. 10 heading for Hurlford and pausing en route for this photograph in the village of Crookedholm, which in those Edwardian times was a coal-mining community. Like all 14 cars in the olive green and cream liveried fleet, this one was constructed by Hurst, Nelson & Co. Ltd. of Motherwell, prominent railway carriage and tramcar builders at that time. Panels around the sides of the top deck were used to advantage by local firms including newsagent Thos. Rodger's bookshop and picture postcard emporium of King Street and Dunlop's cycle agency in John Finnie Street. Due to ever-increasing competition from privately-owned motorbuses in the 1920s, Kilmarnock Corporation replaced their Hurlford tram service with their own buses in 1924, and likewise the cross-town Riccarton to Beansburn tram route in 1926, thus becoming the first Scottish tramway system to close. In 1932 the municipality sold their transport services to the expanding SMT bus group.

Saltcoats railway station about 1920, with the local bus which connected Saltcoats with Stevenston for a fare of 3d. This was SD 3375, a GMC operated by MacGregor of Saltcoats (now a partner in Clyde Coast Services and based in Ardrossan). The scene is little changed today, although the station buildings now lie empty.

G & S.W. Station, Saltcoats.

At the same location in 1990, 70 years later. ECS 56V was a Volvo–Ailsa delivered to A1 service member T. & E. Docherty of Irvine in 1979. These buses were built at Volvo's bus and truck plant in Irvine which provided much-needed local employment from 1967 until 2000 when its closure ended Ayrshire's remaining manufacturing link with the motor industry (Stonefield trucks had been built at Cumnock between 1978 and 1980).

James McKerrow of Largs operated the grandly named 'Largs and West Coast Motor Service' from Largs to Wemyss Bay and Gourock and Largs to Fairlie until selling out to the Greenock & Port Glasgow Tramways Co. in 1913, thus allowing a through service to run between Greenock and Largs via Gourock and Inverkip, and providing the original basis of the service that Western SMT eventually operated between Kilmarnock and Greenock. This scene shows McKerrow's Albion SD 421 (named 'Scotia') leading a long line of similar charabancs and Argyll taxi cabs about 1909.

Probably the first totally enclosed buses in Ayrshire were operated by the Glasgow & South Western Railway Company in connection with their own trains. These were three Milnes–Daimlers (SD 503–4–5) which ran on an hourly frequency between Kilwinning and Ardrossan from June 1906 until the service prematurely ended in October 1907. Bodywork with seating capacity for 21 passengers and rooftop luggage area was built by London coachbuilder Christopher Dodson. SD 504 is seen at Ardrossan.

Thos. Lees was proprietor of the King's Arms Hotel, Girvan, during the Edwardian years of the early twentieth century. He also operated horse-drawn coaches to carry holidaymakers on a circular tour from Girvan to Ballantrae via Lendalfoot and the shore, returning inland via Colmonell, and in 1906 introduced this Sheffield-built Durham–Churchill charabanc on the tour. The tiered bench seating had been patented by Lees, allowing each row of passengers to see over the heads of those in front and had also been fitted to the horse coaches. (Another Girvan firm which operated similar tours from the town was Gray and Young.)

Possibly the earliest example of motorised public transport in Ayrshire was operated in the final years of Queen Victoria's reign by pioneer motor manufacturer John Stirling. He ran Daimler wagonettes with solid tyres, chain drive and tiller steering in various Scottish towns. These were assembled and bodied at his own factory in Hamilton. This example operated between Prestwick, Ayr and Burns' Monument. Seen outside the Burns' Monument Hotel in 1899, it bears the fleet number 4 encircled by a garter with the name Glasgow & West of Scotland Motor Car Co. Ltd., which was presumably one of Stirling's subsidiary companies. Ayr's municipal tramways also operated on this route, but did not commence until 1901.

In the years before regular daily bus services were introduced in the mid-1920s, it was often the local village carrier who operated a service – usually on Saturdays only – into the nearest town. Sometimes the vehicle would run as a lorry during the week and was fitted with a charabanc body for the weekend. Occasionally some owners who did not own a charabanc body simply tied or bolted wooden benches to the platform body on their lorry – and nobody complained because they had not experienced anything better! The example shown here was fitted with a 'chara' body typical of the late Edwardian era prior to the 1914–1918 war. This was SD 571, a solid-tyred chain-driven Albion with canvas side curtains which could be lowered to provide protection in wet or windy weather. It was owned by A. Watson & Sons of Joppa, Coylton and operated from there to Ayr on market days and Saturdays.

Richard Johnstone of Fenwick made the natural progression from horse to motorised transport during the Edwardian era and this Star, seen outside Laigh Cottage, Low Fenwick, was one of the first buses in North Ayrshire. It was popularly known locally as 'Stourie Aggie' because of the clouds of dust it stirred up as it rumbled along the then rutted road to Killie. This name was later applied to other buses in Ayrshire but Dick Johnstone's was the first. Entrance and exit was from a door at the back, while the canvas side curtains could be rolled up as seen here or dropped down during inclement weather. Johnstone continued to operate between Fenwick and Kilmarnock but also commenced a pioneering service linking Kilmarnock, Crosshouse, Dreghorn and Irvine prior to World War I. In 1918 he gave up his haulage and bus interests to start farming at nearby Drumtee. However, his nephew Frank Johnstone then purchased a lorry from his uncle to start a similar transport business on his own account.

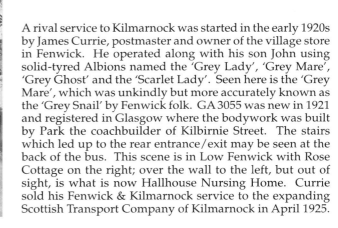

A rival service to Kilmarnock was started in the early 1920s by James Currie, postmaster and owner of the village store in Fenwick. He operated along with his son John using solid-tyred Albions named the 'Grey Lady', 'Grey Mare', 'Grey Ghost' and the 'Scarlet Lady'. Seen here is the 'Grey Mare', which was unkindly but more accurately known as the 'Grey Snail' by Fenwick folk. GA 3055 was new in 1921 and registered in Glasgow where the bodywork was built by Park the coachbuilder of Kilbirnie Street. The stairs which led up to the rear entrance/exit may be seen at the back of the bus. This scene is in Low Fenwick with Rose Cottage on the right; over the wall to the left, but out of sight, is what is now Hallhouse Nursing Home. Currie sold his Fenwick & Kilmarnock service to the expanding Scottish Transport Company of Kilmarnock in April 1925.

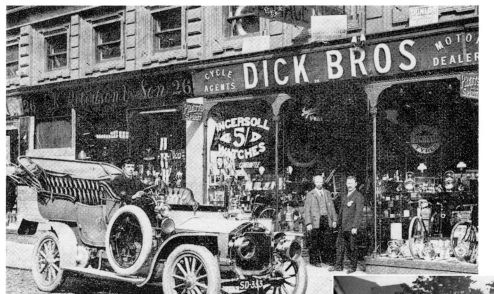

One of the best-known names in the motor trade in the county was that of Dick Bros., Kilmarnock. Like many other garages, the business had originated as a cycle dealer and progressed to mechanised transport as motors slowly gained popularity from the late 1890s onwards. Matthew, David and Douglas Dick opened their first premises in 1895 in John Finnie Street, shortly followed by another warehouse in Duke Street. This view shows SD 333, a 28 h.p. Albion car at Dick Brothers' second Duke Street shop about 1905. At that time the cycle agency was still an important part of the business.

SD 9612 was a 4-ton, 32 h.p, solid-tyred chain-driven Albion A10 lorry supplied by the Ayrshire Albion agent Dick Bros. of Kilmarnock in June 1925 to Rankin & Borland, aerated water manufacturers of East George Street, Kilmarnock. Edwardian advertisements for Rankin & Borland (who had originated as manufacturing chemists and diversified to lemonade production in the mid-nineteenth century) advised the public that in addition to selling lemonade and ginger ale from their shop in King Street, they also supplied trusses, enemas, hot water bottles, water cushions, elastic stockings, knee caps and bandages. Rankin & Borland had been established in 1798, just two years after the death of Robert Burns, and remained a familiar name in the town until the 1950s.

William Young & Sons, who had previously operated bus services in the Bathgate area, came to Ayr in 1923 where they started the Ayr & District Motor Service from their bus station and garage in Fullarton Street, serving a variety of destinations including Cumnock, Burnfoot, Muirkirk, Sanquhar, Annbank, Dunure, Galston and Tarbolton. Services to many of these places also ran from Kilmarnock. A&DMS initially concentrated on Commer buses, later favouring AECs. This picture shows SD 7731, a 1924 Commer Car, as those vehicles were then known, which toppled over an embankment after leaving the road while in service between Kilmarnock and Mauchline. In 1932 Ayr & District sold their operations to the newly-formed Western SMT Co. Ltd.

Kilmarnock's town centre has been altered considerably – some would say architecturally vandalised – since the redevelopment of the 1970s. One area which suffered particularly was Portland Street and this scene shows what was probably the best-known building in that street. This was the bus station, which was opened in October 1923 by the Scottish Transport Company, a predecessor of the Western SMT Co. Ltd. The company was rapidly expanding at this time, with other bus stations built in Ardrossan and Ayr shortly after. In this mid-1920s view some of the drivers and conductresses may be seen in their lightweight summer uniforms and white-topped caps. The buses are all Leylands and from the left are respectively bound for Stewarton, Glasgow, Darvel and Fenwick.

The large Scottish Transport fleet was home to many Leyland buses, most of which were fitted with solid tyres up until the mid-1920s and later converted to pneumatics. SD 8468 was new in 1925 and is seen near Waterside en route from Dalmellington to Ayr. Judging by the number of children on board it would appear that the local school had just closed for the day. The conductress is holding her rack of multicoloured tickets which would be cancelled appropriately with the ticket punch carried on the strap around her neck. The 'Transport' fleet was painted in an attractive deep red livery described by the company as vermilion.

Cross Street in Galston about 1950 showing what was at that time the Queen Mary Café but is now the 'Looking Glass' florists. Heading from Kilmarnock to Darvel and approaching the bus stop at the café is BCS 429, one of a large fleet of Daimlers which entered service sporting gold-topped radiators with the 'Western' in 1948. Bodywork on this one was built by Northern Counties of Wigan, a company which continued to enjoy a long relationship with Western SMT through the years ahead. Back in the 1920s, a locally-based bus operator who provided a service into Killie was Forsyth of Galston. The route between Darvel and Killie was one of the most lucrative in the county for the busmen and at that period even attracted operators from outwith Ayrshire, for instance Sanderson Bros. of Glasgow and Rae of Shotts. Both these firms opened small offices in Kilmarnock.

The Irvine valley towns of Galston, Newmilns and Darvel were originally linked by the railway line to Kilmarnock until closure of its passenger services in 1964. Regular timetabled bus services in the valley were provided from the mid-1920s onwards by both the A1 association for a few years and also by the Scottish General Transport Company, which from 1923 had its headquarters based in Kilmarnock. Simply known by local folk as 'the Transport' (and by some even to this day!), this company operated the first double-deckers in Ayrshire. These were Leyland Titan TD1s with open staircase bodywork, also built by Leyland as exemplified here by AG 2526. This was the first to be delivered and is seen when new in 1928 at Hastings Square in Darvel. Already it has an almost full complement of passengers setting off for Kilmarnock on what was almost certainly a Saturday afternoon. The driver was Edward (Ned) Nairn who continued to drive with Western SMT for many years.

Approaching the end of its journey up the valley from Kilmarnock to Darvel in 1937 is one of many second-hand double deckers acquired by the Western SMT Co. during the 1930s. Leyland Titan WE 3686 had commenced life with Sheffield Corporation in 1928 and then operated with Western from 1936 until 1948. A message boy on his delivery bike with wicker basket leads the way as the bus passes the town hall opposite Hastings Square. A Ford model 'Y' of the mid-1930s is parked near the bus stop while on the other side of the street is the now-closed Co-operative store.

Looking down Glaisnock Street, Cumnock in the late 1930s, while a boy on his bike waits for the approaching Western SMT bus to pass. This was Leyland Lion VD 792, liveried in the company's smart black and white colours. It climbs past the Western depot (now a funeral parlour) which had been opened in 1923 by the Ayr & District Motor Service Company and used by them until acquisition by Western in 1932. A horse and cart makes it way downhill into town.

Western's new bus depot in Ayr Road, Cumnock replaced the congested Glaisnock Street garage in 1954. Leaving to take up service 5 to Glasgow in the early 1960s is 1532, an Alexander-bodied Leyland PD3 (MSD 396). These premises are now occupied by Stagecoach buses who took over from Western in 1994.

Girvan North Parish Church is seen in the background of this photograph of Church Square at Montgomerie Street. Both buses were imported American Reos in the fleet of Ayrshire Pullman Motor Services of Smith Street, Ayr, who ran – as may be seen from the window bills – from Ayr to Girvan via Alloway, Maybole, Kirkoswald, Maidens and Turnberry. The 14-seat charabanc was AG 481, known as the 'Yellow Peril' because of its livery, while the saloon was GD 1343, which had been the first bus in the Pullman fleet, bought in December 1925, and painted chocolate brown. Ayrshire Pullman was owned by David Ritchie, manager of the Dalmellington Coal Company and his son-in-law Tom McGawn was in charge. In 1927 the Girvan service was extended to Ballantrae and in 1928 a twice-daily Ayr–Girvan–Newton Stewart service started. The following year the LMS Railway Co. took control and in 1931 the operation passed to the predatory SMT Company of Edinburgh who transferred it to their newly formed subsidiary Western SMT in 1932.

Day and half-day tours from Girvan continued to be operated into the 1960s by Western SMT, but this scene at the harbour stance was taken in 1938 and shows CS 4717, a Duple-bodied Bedford 20-seater with sliding roof. The traditional tour boards offer two afternoon excursions – a circular to Burns' Monument via Maybole, Dunure and the 'Electric Brae' and a trip to Ballantrae following the same popular route as Thos. Lee's horse-drawn coaches had taken in the early 1900s – via Kennedy's Pass and Colmonell in the Stinchar valley. The fare for each tour was 2/6, or half a crown as this sum was usually known.

The attractive village of Straiton was first connected by a regular bus service to Ayr in the early 1920s. This was thanks to James Murray McGill of the Commercial Hotel, King Street, Crosshill, whose 'Carrick Pullman' service originally ran a model 'T' Ford to connect with the trains at Maybole station and later extended to Ayr. A summer extension at the other end of the route served the then popular picnic spot at Tairlaw Linn. This view of Straiton Main Street in 1927 looking towards the monument on the summit of Craigengower (top right) shows Albion AG 1796 outside the Black Bull Hotel. McGill sold the Carrick services to the expanding Western SMT Company in 1932 and moved to Barrhead in Renfrewshire where he took over O'Hara's bus service to Paisley, which the family continued to operate until 1997 when Arriva acquired the business.

VA 7215 (fleet no. 177) was one of many Albions in John Sword's 'Midland' Bus Service of Airdrie. J. C. Sword became general manager of Western SMT when that company was formed in 1932. This 1929 scene in Dalry shows driver Hector Fraser with his bus on the lengthy journey from Ayr to Airdrie via Troon, Irvine, Kilwinning, Dalry, Beith, Johnstone, Paisley, Glasgow and Coatbridge. The bodywork on this 1927 bus was built by Midland in their Airdrie workshops to replace the original which had been badly damaged in a road accident near Coatbridge. Although most of the fleet carried a red livery, others, like 177, operated with unpainted aluminium panels with a sandpapered thumbed design. The inset advert appeared in 1928.

The bus station in Boswell Park, Ayr, which was opened in 1931 by AA Motor Services Ltd., photographed in 1935 during celebrations of the 25th year of King George V's reign. Albions, four of which are seen here, were the mainstay of the fleet at this time (the livery of which was then red, not changing to the more familiar green until post-war). The three to the left (AG 4054, AG 3987, XS 2476) with their engines projecting from the front are what is known as normal control or bonnet type while the one on the right (AG 7747) is forward control, that is with the driver sitting in his own cab alongside the engine. The adverts on the hoardings in the background are also interesting. One is for a football match between Ayr United and Galston and others include names which are familiar to this day such as Mars bars, Whitbread stout, Guinness, Andrew's Liver Salt and Capstan cigarettes. A mysterious poster on the billboards refers to 'The war of 1938'. One of the members of AA (Ayr–Ardrossan) Motor Services was Dodds of Troon who are still in business today as coach hirers, although now based in East Road, Ayr.

The former Ayr municipal tramway depots on both sides of Bellesleyhill Road at its junction with Prestwick Road, Newton Park, became the garages for Western SMT buses from 1932 until ever-increasing shortage of space demanded a new depot which was opened at Waggon Road in 1952. This wartime view looking towards Prestwick shows the cramped erstwhile tramway premises with the tracks still visible leading through the forecourt. All the Western buses were painted in the black and white livery which had been introduced in 1937 and the fleet included an assortment of second-hand Leylands and Albions. The site of the Newton Park premises is now occupied by the Kwik Save foodstore and Furniture World.

Kilmarnock was one of the few towns in Scotland which for many years boasted two bus stations. The main one in Portland Street, as seen on page 16, was owned for most of its life by the Western SMT Co. Ltd. whose services radiated from there to most parts of the county. However, the A1 Bus Owners' Association, serving the route to Crosshouse, Springside, Dreghorn, Irvine, Kilwinning, Stevenston, Saltcoats and Ardrossan also had bus station premises, first in St Marnock Street and then from 1959, as seen above, at John Dickie Street. When the town centre was redeveloped the present bus station was built in Green Street with sufficient space for both operators (who are now under the ownership of the giant Stagecoach group). This view of the former A1 bus station shows a Leyland PD2 to the right, while in the foreground are two former London Transport vehicles. JXN 341 was a Leyland RTL owned by A1 member Ian Duff of Parkhouse Garage, Ardrossan, while JXC 165 was an AEC RT type belonging to James Murray of Saltcoats. Buses were bought from London Transport by several of the A1 owners during the 1950s and 1960s and served the company well for many years.

A fine summer day in 1935. One can almost hear the Albion Valiant toiling in low gear up the Haylie Brae from Largs. It has its sliding roof opened fully, allowing the passengers to enjoy the sunshine and fresh air on their journey to Kilbirnie, Johnstone, Paisley and Glasgow. The bus was XS 3494, one of an almost 100% fleet of Albions owned by Young's Bus Service of Paisley who had pioneered this route in the mid-1920s. Young's service also connected Glasgow with West Kilbride and an extension during summer months to Seamill. Beyond Largs, the northern tip of the Isle of Cumbrae may be seen to the left, while Bute lies across the Firth of Clyde. The location of this photograph was not far from the former 'Bonny Blink' tearoom, where customers could enjoy this unrivalled view.

The tiny village of Portencross lies 3 miles north-west of West Kilbride at Farland Head, on the promontory which forms the westernmost point of Ayrshire's Cunninghame coastline. Its pier was a port of call for paddle steamers prior to the Great War (and again briefly in the 1990s when *Waverley* called in). In 1923, when this photograph was taken, it was a much livelier community than today. Charabancs brought day trippers to picnic by the shore and historic castle while refreshments could be purchased at the post office tearooms, seen in the background. An elderly couple, accompanied by their little terrier, drive away from the village in SD 5345, their brand new Swift two-seater. Since few ordinary folk could afford the luxury of even a modest car such as this at that period, perhaps the owner was a professional gentleman. Swifts were popular cars in the 1920s and relatively inexpensive, but like so many other marques were unable to compete with the increasingly mass-produced opposition, and so the Coventry-based company went out of business in 1931.

Ayr High Street has always been a lively place; this 1938 view shows it from the junction with Kyle and Alloway streets. YS 7, on the left, is a smart 3½ litre Bentley of 1935 with a locally registered (CS) Standard parked in front. Another Ayrshire car is CS 7001, a Ford 8 of 1937 disappearing towards the Wallace Tower, while approaching is a Vauxhall Big 6 followed by a Hillman. Parked adjacent to Homer McCririck's well-known bookshop and newsagents is HH 4982, a 1929 Guy lorry owned by W. B. Anderson & Sons Ltd. There have been many changes over the years among the High Street shops. For instance, the Kilmarnock Equitable Co-operative Society on the left is now occupied by the Woolwich Building Society, while on the right Audrey's ladies shop is now the Moben/Dolphin kitchen and bathroom store. The Fifty Shilling Tailor in Victoria Buildings is now Jeanster, but at least the old-established Tam O' Shanter Inn remains the same.

The caravan site at Maidens beach was a popular spot for many visitors from near and far. This scene from around 1930 shows GE 3072, a 1928 wire-wheeled Standard 18/36 h.p. saloon which has pulled the family caravan from Glasgow. Car, caravan and tent were owned by A. K. Stevenson of Glasgow (originally from Kilwinning), who for many years was secretary of the Royal Scottish Automobile Club in Blythswood Square.

SEAMILL BEACH AND ARRAN HILLS   A.2272

Another popular Ayrshire beach was at Seamill looking over the Firth of Clyde towards the hills on the Isle of Arran. Today proper car parking areas are laid out adjacent to the beach, but this mid-1930s scene shows how motorists of the time simply parked on the sands. Amongst the selection of typical saloon cars of the period are SN 2984, a Dunbartonshire-registered two-seat Morris Cowley open tourer of 1925, with its 'dickey' seat open, while alongside is XS 3709, a Paisley-registered Morris 8 saloon, with father resting on the running board.

Finlay Dickson's garage and petrol station in Rigg Street, Stewarton was typical of many where the owner had his family home above the premises. Dickson's brother-in-law John Boyle had been the previous proprietor of this Ford agency in the 'bonnet town'. The year was 1929, when apple green Ford AG 4120 was new; it was a model 'A' Tudor (signifying two door) as opposed to the Fordor (four door model). The first Ford to be produced after the famous model 'T', it was fitted with a conventional gearbox, unlike the Tin Lizzie's pre-select system. This photo shows Finlay Dickson himself along with his son John and Fido. Also noteworthy is the Pratt's 'Ethyl' petrol bowser which swung out from the wall, and – just decipherable on the sliding door – one of the once-familiar circular AA road signs which informed motorists of their whereabouts. This one is of course for Stewarton and shows the distance to Kilmarnock as 5 miles and Dunlop 2½. Latterly this business was owned by McFadzean's but the building was demolished in the 1990s to make way for redevelopment, a filling station still occupying part of the site.

One of the best collections of veteran and vintage cars in the British Isles was owned by John C. Sword of East Balgray Farm by Torranyard. John Sword had started a garage business in Airdrie in 1920 and soon afterwards commenced bus operations under the name of Midland Bus Services, building up a network of routes in Lanarkshire, Renfrewshire and Ayrshire. Midland subsequently merged with the infant Scottish Motor Traction Company and Mr Sword was appointed general manager and director of the newly formed Western SMT Co. Ltd. in 1932. John Sword's other great interest was aviation, and in 1933 he commenced air services with the Midland & Scottish Air Ferries from Renfrew to the Western Isles, also operating the famous air ambulance flights with De Haviland Dragons. This view at Prestwick Airport in the late 1960s shows a Barker-bodied Rolls Royce 40/50 h.p. Silver Ghost which had formerly been part of John Sword's collection of early automobiles, but had originally been owned by the Marquis of Bute in 1908. After Sword's death in 1960, the car collection was sold at two auctions and this Rolls achieved the highest price (£7,200) at the 1965 sale. Incidentally, the Bedford van seen in front of the VC10 was used at Prestwick for providing the hot air necessary to start up the aircraft engines.

Like so many other companies in Ayrshire, indeed throughout Scotland, James Morrison & Sons Ltd. chose Albion Motors for their delivery fleet. Albions, built in Scotstoun, Glasgow, were famed for their reliability; in fact the company advertising slogan was 'Sure as the Sunrise'. This was a 24 h.p 30 cwt. van purchased in May 1924 by Morrison, who had bakers shops in Fullarton Place and Shore Road, Stevenston. The photograph was taken prior to delivery of the van and it had not been given a registration mark at this stage.

AG 7178 was a Commer lorry bought new by haulage contractors and coal merchants James and Archibald Fulton of Crosshouse in 1932. Standing proudly alongside is driver James Fulton, while the 'lorry boys' are unknown. On this occasion the Commer was engaged on coal deliveries around the doors in Crosshouse. A. & J. Fulton is still a well-known name in road haulage circles in Scotland and successfully continues as a general haulier in the increasingly difficult business environment of the twenty-first century, having been in existence since 1920 in the days of mainly horse-drawn transport (Fulton's used horse-drawn wagons alongside their motor lorries until the late 1930s). This Commer would have been painted in the same blue and red livery that is used today on the Fulton fleet, which is still based at their original site in Main Street, Crosshouse.

The Hosiery Manufacturing Co. Ltd. was founded in 1904 by James Watson at 30 Ballot Road, Irvine where it remains to this day, although now known as HMC Holdings Ltd. and no longer producing knitwear. Sadly none of the thirteen firms which were once involved in the knitwear industry in the town now exist, all having found it impossible to compete in today's financial climate. At least HMC has survived, albeit having diversified into general storage and distribution. SD 7722 was an Albion van bought by the company in 1923, mainly for delivering knitwear products from their factories in Irvine and Troon to railway stations for onward transport to customers throughout Britain (there was also a thriving export trade to 27 countries worldwide). It was a 24 h.p. 2-tonner with solid tyres which also delivered to some of the company's 60 retail outlets. These 'wool shops' displayed the same once-familiar 'washing line' logo as may be seen on the van.

CS 4660, a 9-ton six-wheeler Albion, was supplied to haulage contractors Hugh & David Gillespie of Girdle Toll in 1936. Albion Motors had used the vehicle for exhibition purposes on their stand at the Scottish Motor Show at the Kelvin Hall in Glasgow that year, prior to delivery to Gillespies. Bodywork on the lorry was built by Robert Rogerson, whose premises were adjacent to the Albion Works at Scotstoun and who naturally built many bodies on Albion chassis.

This style of articulated 'bin lorry', as we usually referred to them, was popular with many local authorities throughout Scotland. The Royal Burgh of Ayr operated this Scammell 3-ton mechanical horse during the 1930s and 1940s at which time William B. Strain was director of the municipal cleansing department. The special refuse body was built by Laurie of Falkirk who specialised in this type of vehicle.

Just like Johnnie Walker, Clark & Co.'s shoe business had been founded in Kilmarnock in 1820. In its heyday in the 1950s, Clark's Saxone shoes had well over 1,000 employees at their Gleneagles works in Mill Street. This Stockport-registered Albion Chieftain delivery van was purchased in 1952.

McCall & Greenshields were well-known haulage contractors in Kilmarnock and were based at Wallacehill, Riccarton. Like so many other contractors in the area most of their loads were sourced either from the various local engineering works (Glenfield & Kennedy provided much custom) or from a large number of farms in the surrounding country districts. McCall & Greenshields used the slogan 'Any load if there's a road'. Close inspection of the above photograph shows that this Albion Chieftain of 1952 was named 'Wallacehill Superb' as most of the lorry fleet bore individual names.

Johnnie Walker's slogan 'Born 1820 – still going strong' with the logo depicting a Regency dandy in top hat, breeches, boots, cane and a quizzing glass was the work of Edwardian artist Tom Browne. The famous figure may be seen astride the headboard of this Albion Victor 4 cylinder diesel which was new to the whisky delivery fleet in 1959 and is seen here near the Dick Institute in Kilmarnock. NAG 328 had a cab by Homalloy and is still in existence since it has been restored for preservation by Ayrshire commercial vehicle enthusiast Frank MacDougall.

Young Bros. of Galston purchased this Albion Clydesdale registered RAG 244 in 1960 for milk collection around Ayrshire farms. The 1,750 gallon milk tank was constructed by appropriately named W. P. Butterfield Ltd. of Shipley, Yorkshire. Young Bros. were also general haulage contractors and additionally members of the A1 Bus Owners Association. In 1962 the business was sold to Jas. McKinnon Jnr. of Kilmarnock.

Alexander Frew is still in business today in Boglemart Street, Stevenston, as coal merchant and haulage contractor, after trading for over a century. Horse-drawn wagons were originally used for coal deliveries and carriages were also supplied for funerals and general hire. Diversification came during the early 1920s when a small motorbus was operated in competition with several others between Saltcoats and Stevenston. This photo was taken at the now-demolished Ardeer Recreation Hall on Stevenston gala day during Queen Elizabeth's Coronation year in 1953. Suitably decorated for the occasion are SE 5711, an example of the wartime square-nosed OY-type Bedford and former US army Chevrolet AAG 744 with specially painted white-wall tyres. (Photo by Tom Frew.)

Most of us remember the mobile shops which were operated by the Co-operative movement in all parts of the country (many will probably still recall their dividend number too). In particular, they were a boon to small rural communities and also outlying housing schemes which lacked the benefits of good shopping facilities. This one was owned by Dalmellington Co-op, whose registered office was in High Main Street. Albions were the most popular chassis for Co-op societies and Dalmellington was no exception; CSD 337 was a 6 cylinder petrol engined FT3 model new in 1949.

Prestwick Airport was founded by Scottish Aviation in 1935 and was Scotland's major international gateway for many years. The Prestwick Pioneer, the little aircraft which needed no airfields, was built here, but land transport was also constructed by Scottish Aviation. From 1948 until 1952 both single and double deck bus bodies were produced and then in the mid-1960s an attempt at building battery-powered cars unfortunately proved unsuccessful. The Scamp, as it was appropriately named (combining its Scottish parentage with the fact that it was an electric vehicle), reached a production total of about a dozen only. It certainly had no problems parking, as is evident from the photo of DAG 908C, one of the earliest models of 1965 with 'cyclops eye' style headlight.

Later Scamps with the more conventional style of lighting design are seen here under construction at Prestwick.

Heads of Ayr station lost its services twice. The first time was in 1930 when the Glasgow & South Western Railway also withdrew passenger facilities at Maidens and Dunure. The second Heads of Ayr station, as seen here, was built to serve the nearby naval training base during the 1939–1945 war. After hostilities ended, Butlin's holiday camp was established on the site and the station enjoyed a new lease of life serving holidaymakers until final closure in 1968. This view shows BR Class 2P 4-4-0 loco 40610 arriving under the watchful eye of the local stationmaster in July 1958. For several summer seasons a welcoming piper met the trains and marched at the head of the incoming holidaymakers down to Butlin's camp.

Dalmellington railway station about 1920. Solid-tyred Albion SD 1235 awaits custom from train passengers about to arrive. It was owned by James MacDonald, proprietor of the Eglinton Hotel, Dalmellington, who is seen here with what was then his newest charabanc. In conjunction with the Glasgow & South Western Railway he had operated tourist services to Carsphairn, New Galloway and Dalry (Kirkcudbrightshire) since about 1908, advertised as 'Land of Crockett' excursions. Several enamel advertising signs which were once so common at railway stations are visible, viz.: National crude oil engines, 'self starting from cold, low consumption of cheap oils'; Virol, 'growing boys need it' and 'Wincarnis' are represented, while Affleck's house furnishers of Ayr High Street promote their settees, easy chairs, carpets and curtains.

Dalmellington station closed in April 1964. For the final few years prior to this date, small railbuses like this were able to cope with the reduced public patronage. Local folk who lived in the large council scheme at Bellsbank or in Burnton had much easier access to the bus service to and from Ayr provided by Western SMT and so the declining passenger traffic spiralled even lower. The use of railbuses could not stem this decline and merely cut operational costs. The writing was on the wall for the line which had opened to passengers back in 1856 but had almost always carried more coals than souls. This scene in May 1962 shows AC Cars railbus no. SC 79979 about to leave with the 6.25 p.m. for Ayr. (Photo by W. A. C. Smith.)

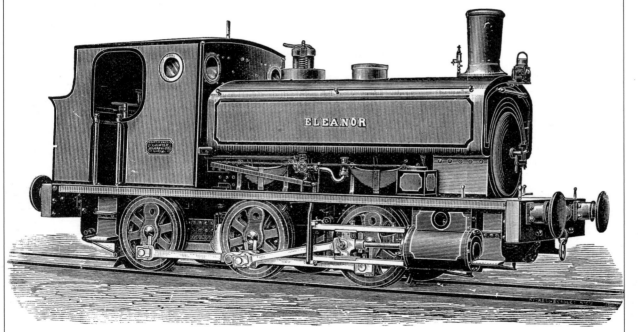
Today the sole survivor from all the railway locomotive builders once found in Scotland is Andrew Barclay (now Hunslet–Barclay) of Kilmarnock. In Killie alone there were formerly several rival railway loco builders. Barclay built the first steam locomotive at his Caledonia Works in 1859 for the Portland Iron Co. of Hurlford and went on to specialise in the construction of railway engines mainly for industrial sites in both the UK and overseas. A typical example is seen in this advert from 1892 which shows an 0-6-0 Barclay tank engine named *Eleanor* which is believed to have been supplied to the Wearmouth Coal Company of Co. Durham. Working examples of Barclay-built locos may still be seen today at the Scottish Industrial Railway Centre (operated by the enthusiastic members of the Ayrshire Railway Preservation Group) at Minnivey, Dalmellington.